IT'S TIME TO LEARN ABOUT ARCHAEOPTERYX

It's Time to Learn about Archaeopteryx

Walter the Educator

Silent King Books
A WhichHead Entertainment Imprint

Copyright © 2025 by Walter the Educator

All rights reserved. No part of this book may be reproduced in any manner whatsoever without written per- mission except in the case of brief quotations embodied in critical articles and reviews.

First Printing, 2024

Disclaimer

This book is a literary work; the story is not about specific persons, locations, situations, and/or circumstances unless mentioned in a historical context. Any resemblance to real persons, locations, situations, and/or circumstances is coincidental. This book is for entertainment and informational purposes only. The author and publisher offer this information without warranties expressed or implied. No matter the grounds, neither the author nor the publisher will be accountable for any losses, injuries, or other damages caused by the reader's use of this book. The use of this book acknowledges an understanding and acceptance of this disclaimer.

It's Time to Learn about Archaeopteryx is a collectible early learning book by Walter the Educator suitable for all ages belonging to Walter the Educator's Time to Eat Book Series. Collect more books at WaltertheEducator.com

USE THE EXTRA SPACE TO TAKE NOTES AND DOCUMENT YOUR MEMORIES

ARCHAEOPTERYX

Long ago, in times so old,

It's Time to Learn about
Archaeopteryx

A creature lived both fierce and bold.

With wings like birds and claws so strong,

It soared and scurried all day long!

Archaeopteryx, can you say?

It lived in times so far away!

A mix of bird and dino too,

With feathers bright and teeth that chew.

It wasn't big, it wasn't tall,

About the size of crows so small.

With feathered wings but claws to grip,

It ran and flapped but didn't skip!

Unlike the birds we see today,

It had some teeth to catch its prey.

With jaws so sharp and eyes so keen,

It hunted bugs in forests green.

It's Time to Learn about
Archaeopteryx

Its feathers helped it glide with ease,

Between the branches, through the trees.

Not quite flying, not too slow,

It used the wind to help it go!

With hollow bones and tail so long,

It balanced well but wasn't strong.

Though it could leap and flutter high,

It couldn't soar across the sky.

Archaeopteryx tells the tale,

Of how birds' traits began to sail.

From dinosaurs to flapping wings,

This fossil showed so many things!

Found in stone so hard and gray,

Its shape was saved to this very day.

Scientists cheered, what did they find?

It's Time to Learn about
Archaeopteryx

A link to birds, a clue to time!

So when you see a bird in flight,

Think of this old fossil bright.

For long ago, before our view,

It lived in forests warm and new!

Archaeopteryx, a name so long,

But now you know its special song.

A mix of old, a mix of new,

It's Time to Learn about Archaeopteryx

A wondrous creature, strange but true!

ABOUT THE CREATOR

Walter the Educator is one of the pseudonyms for Walter Anderson. Formally educated in Chemistry, Business, and Education, he is an educator, an author, a diverse entrepreneur, and he is the son of a disabled war veteran. "Walter the Educator" shares his time between educating and creating. He holds interests and owns several creative projects that entertain, enlighten, enhance, and educate, hoping to inspire and motivate you. Follow, find new works, and stay up to date with Walter the Educator™

at WaltertheEducator.com

www.ingramcontent.com/pod-product-compliance
Lightning Source LLC
LaVergne TN
LVHW052017060526
838201LV00059B/4067